Natural Disas

FLOODS AND TIDAL WAVES

Terry Jennings

Belitha Press

First published in Great Britain in 1999 by

Belitha Press
A member of **Chrysalis** Books plc
64 Brewery Road, London, N7 9NT

Paperback edition first published in 2003

Copyright © Belitha Press Limited 1999
Text copyright © Terry Jennings 1999

Produced for Belitha Press Limited by Bender Richardson White
Project editor: Lionel Bender
Project production: Kim Richardson
Designer: Ben White
Text editor: Clare Oliver
Electronic make–up: Mike Weintroub
Illustrator: Rudi Vizi
Picture researchers: Cathy Stastny and Daniela Marceddu
Consultant: Stephen Watts

ISBN 1 84138 046 6 (hb)
ISBN 1 84138 758 4 (pb)

Printed in Hong Kong.
10 9 8 7 6 5 4 3 2 1 (hb)
10 9 8 7 6 5 4 3 2 1 (pb)

British Library Cataloguing in Publication Data
CIP data for this book is available from the British Library

Photographic credits
Panos Pictures: 4 J. Hartley, 5t Jean-Léo Dugast, 8b Jim Holmes, 21 Zed Nelson. **Still Pictures:** 5b Peter Frischmuth, 6 G. Griffiths-Christian Aid, 14 Jim Wark, 17t Hartmut Schwarzbach, 26 Jim Wark, 28t & 28b Mark Edwards. **Tony Stone Images:** 7, 9t Thierry Borredon, 11 Vince Streano, front cover and 18 Ken Biggs. **Rex Features:** 10t & 10b. **Corbis Images:** 13t Scott T. Smith, 13b Robert Holmes, 15 David Rubinger. **Terry Jennings:** 17b, 22b, 24t. **Gamma/Frank Spooner Pictures:** 1 & 22t Thierry Falise, 19 Hokkaido Newspaper, 27 R. Nickelsberg. **Environmental Images:** back cover and 20 Jim Holmes. **Oxford Scientific Films**: 24b Jim Hallett.

Words in **bold** appear in the glossary on pages 30 and 31.

Contents

Floods

All rivers **flood** from time to time. Very heavy rain or rapidly melting snow may produce more water than a river can hold. When this happens, the water spills over the **banks** and spreads across the low-lying land near the river.

Causes of flooding

In many places people have made flooding worse. They have cut down forests on the slopes near rivers. This makes rainwater run off the surface of the land quickly. People also build houses on the flat land near river banks, and so put themselves directly at risk from flooding. Rainfall and rivers are one cause of flooding. Wind and sea are another. If a strong wind blows towards the land when there is a high **tide**, serious flooding of coastal areas may occur. Sometimes **volcanoes** and **earthquakes** under the sea produce gigantic waves that sweep ashore.

▼ *The flooded city of Khartoum, Sudan. Even places that are normally dry can suffer sudden floods.*

Useful and harmful floods

Floods can cause great damage and loss of life. They wash away **beaches** and destroy farmland. They damage buildings and kill or injure people. But river floods are sometimes useful. When a river floods, water pours over its banks, spreading mud and sand over the land. This mud and sand makes very **fertile** soil for growing food crops.

Looking at floods

In this book, we find out what causes floods and how floods change the landscape. We look at how floods damage property and endanger people. We also see what can be done to prevent flooding.

▲ *Some areas flood so often that the people who live there build their houses on stilts. This farmhouse is on the Irrawaddy Delta in Myanmar.*

▼ *In Wertheim-am-Martin, Germany, a rescue worker pulls flood victims to safety in a dinghy.*

Why rivers flood

◄ *Unexpected, heavy rains swell the River Tana in eastern Kenya. Suddenly, there was too much water for the river to hold and it flooded nearby villages.*

A river floods when heavy rainfall or melting snow produces more water than the river can hold. A river may also flood if it becomes blocked. As a river nears a **lake** or the sea, its **valley** is wide and flat. When the river floods, this is the first place where water pours over its banks. The worst floods usually happen in tropical regions, where winds called **monsoons** bring heavy rains.

Heavy rainstorms

Many parts of the world have sudden, heavy rainstorms, especially places which receive most of their rain in one short, wet season. The rain swells the rivers and can flood land far away. The regular flooding of the River Ganges near its mouth in Bangladesh is caused by heavy rains far away in the Himalayas.

Ice blockages

Cold parts of the world are hit by floods, too. The longer rivers that flow north to the Arctic Ocean in northern Canada and Russia often flood. In winter, the rivers freeze over. When spring comes, the ice melts in the upper, warmer parts of the river before it melts near the sea. The rivers fill up with all the melted snow from the surrounding area, but in the cold north, the mouths of the rivers are still frozen. When water hits this ice blockage, the river overflows and floods the land.

Rocks and flooding

Some rocks, such as chalk and sandstone, soak up water like a sponge. They are called **permeable** rocks. Other rocks, such as clay and granite, can help to make floods worse. These rocks are called **impermeable**. They do not let water through, so the water runs over their surface and quickly fills up rivers and streams.

Towns and cities have huge areas of concrete and tarmac. These act in the same way as impermeable rocks. Heavy rain runs off the surface into drains, which flow into rivers and streams. The sudden rush of water can make the rivers and streams overflow and cause flooding.

▲ Car parks in large towns and cities are usually covered in concrete or tarmac. These materials do not allow rainwater to soak away into the ground, so the parks can become flooded.

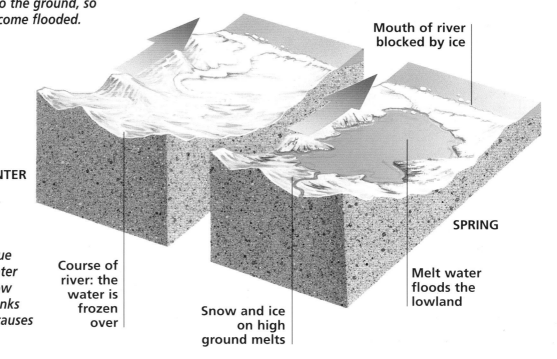

WINTER

SPRING

Mouth of river blocked by ice

Course of river: the water is frozen over

Snow and ice on high ground melts

Melt water floods the lowland

► Ice blocks the mouth of a river. Unable to continue forwards, the water from melting snow spills over the banks of the river and causes flooding.

Useful floods

▼ *The course of a typical river from its beginning, or source, to its mouth on the coast.*

Source

Upper valley

Tributary

Gorge

Waterfall

Oxbow lake

Meander

Flood plain

Delta

Mouth

Estuary

When a river nears the end of its journey – the sea or a lake – it flows across flat lowland. Here, the river tends to wind in big curves. It flows slowly along the curves, which are called **meanders**. This combination of flat land and wide meanders means that the water can spread out across much more land.

Flood plains

The area that would be underwater if a river floods is called its **flood plain**. When a river floods, water pours over its banks, dumping mud and sand over the land. This mud and sand makes a very fertile soil, called **alluvial soil**.

The Nile's flood plain

Ancient Egypt became a wealthy country because of the River Nile's flood plain. Each year the Nile flooded and brought water to land that otherwise had very little rain. It also washed fertile mud on to the river banks. Here people grew cotton, corn for bread, rice, and vegetables. The Egyptians believed the Nile was a god. Some years there were droughts and the Nile did not flood. People thought this was because their god was angry.

Floods in Bangladesh

Most of the country of Bangladesh lies on the fan-shaped area, or **delta**, at the mouths of the Rivers Ganges and Brahmaputra. This flat flood plain is one of the largest in the world. The two great rivers often flood the plain, leaving a layer of fertile mud over the fields.

So long as the monsoon rains fall, up to three crops of rice are grown here in a year. However, in some years the monsoon rains fail to arrive. When this happens, there is a drought and food runs short.

In other years, the rains are very heavy and the flooding is severe. Too much water destroys the crops, and damages buildings, power supplies and roads. In severe floods, many people lose their lives.

▲ Crops still grow well in the fertile, alluvial soil of the Nile valley. In Egypt today, the Aswan Dam prevents the river flooding each year and controls the flow of water to irrigate the land.

◄ These Bangladeshi villagers stand in the flood waters. In their nets they catch fish that have been swept away from the river.

Disasters

▲ *More than five million Chinese soldiers worked to rebuild the banks of the Yangtze to protect a further 200 million people living lower down the river.*

Rather surprisingly, it is slow-rising floods that cause the most deaths and destruction, especially in Asia. In China, for example, if the monsoon rains last longer than usual or are heavier than normal, then flooding almost always follows.

The Yangtze River

The Yangtze is the longest river in China and the fourth-longest river in the world. It starts high in the snow-covered mountains of western China. More than 700 small rivers join the Yangtze on its 6300-kilometre journey across China, before it flows into the East China Sea at Shanghai. Nearly half of the 1.2 billion people of China live near the banks of the Yangtze.

▲ *When the Yangtze flooded in 1998, 3000 people died. This boy from Hubei Province had a lucky escape.*

Forest clearance

In 1998 the Yangtze flooded, as it had done many times in the past. But the 1998 floods lasted longer than ever before. The flooding was caused by exceptionally heavy rains. The results were worse than usual because, over the years, people had cut down the trees on the slopes of the mountains and hills in the upper parts of the river.

The trees had been cleared for timber and firewood, and to make fields for crops. The heavy rainfall was no longer taken up by the roots of trees and other plants. Instead, the water ran straight off the bare slopes into the Yangtze.

Destruction and death

In the 1998 floods, the Yangtze was so swollen with water that it looked like a sea. The river's banks gave way and the flood waters spread out across the surrounding land. Roads were turned into canals, and towns and villages became lakes. Hundreds of villages were destroyed and millions of farmers and their families were left stranded on strips of high ground.

Altogether the flood affected 240 million people, four times the population of Britain. About 3000 people were drowned and millions more were left homeless. The flood put China's most important industries out of action and destroyed the fields where food crops for millions of people were grown. The results of that one flood will affect the people of China for many years to come.

▼ *Slow-rising floods can occur after heavy rain almost anywhere. This storm flooding is in Huntington Beach, California.*

Flash floods

The most spectacular and rapid floods are flash floods. Most are caused when a thunderstorm or **hurricane** brings a short, heavy burst of rain over the mountains. When this happens, the water level in a mountain stream rises very quickly and sends a wall of water rushing as fast as an express train down into the valley below. Other flash floods are caused by the rapid melting of snow, or when a **dam** bursts.

▼ A flash flood is caused when a large amount of rain falls in a short time over a mountainous area.

Hardly any rain soaks into the valley's steep sides

Thunderstorms bring heavy rain

Winds push moist air up the mountains

The water spreads out across the plain, flooding villages

Almost all the rainwater rushes into the mountain stream. A narrow valley channels the water even faster downstream

◄ *A flash flood in a gully sends cascades of muddy water into the River Missouri, Montana, in the United States. In a flash flood, dry earth turns to mud in minutes.*

▼ *Children paddle in the shallows after a flash flood in the Ziz valley, Morocco. Usually this valley is dry and parched.*

Thunderstorm floods

Although few thunderstorms last more than an hour or two, in that time they can release more than 100 million litres of water. This can cause terrible, unexpected flooding.

Biescas, Spain

In August 1996, in the Pyrenees Mountains in northern Spain, a severe thunderstorm broke out one afternoon. The sky went dark, and hailstones the size of golf balls fell. This was followed by 80 millimetres of rain in just two hours. The rain washed soil, stones, boulders and trees into a mountain stream, which quickly became a raging torrent.

Further downstream, artificial drainage channels rapidly filled with water. Suddenly, a giant wall of water crashed down the valley and through a nearby camp site. A total of 87 people died and 180 were injured. Some bodies were found 16 kilometres from the site.

Desert floods

In many desert areas, the ground is baked hard by the sun and the surface becomes like concrete. In heavy rain, the water rushes over the surface, filling gullies and dry river beds in minutes. In the deserts of North America, more people drown in flash floods than die from thirst.

Bursting dams

Another major cause of flash flooding is when a dam bursts. A dam is a large wall or bank built to hold back water. A man-made lake, called a **reservoir**, fills up behind the dam.

Dams are built across river valleys to save up river water for drinking, **irrigating** crops and producing electricity. They can even help stop flooding by holding back the water. But if a dam bursts, it can cause even worse flooding.

▲ Trees, rocks and debris washed away by heavy rains can become trapped by a bridge, forming a temporary dam. The water level rises behind the dam and bridge.

▲ The Glen Canyon Dam in Utah, USA, holds back the waters of Lake Powell. This massive structure is built between the high walls of the valley.

▲ The bridge and temporary dam eventually burst under the pressure, resulting in a flash flood.

The Aznacollar dam burst

One of the worst ever dam bursts was at the Aznacollar iron-ore mine near the south coast of Spain in April 1998. This dam was unusual because the reservoir behind it contained not drinking water but water loaded with poisonous wastes from the mine.

In the early hours of 25 April, the wall of the reservoir burst. This may have been because of a small earthquake in the area. The dam burst released five million cubic litres of water, containing acids and other poisonous substances such as lead, mercury, zinc, cadmium and arsenic on to the surrounding land.

▲ *A road in the Negev Desert, Israel, becomes a river during a flash flood. Heavy rains washed away banks along the roadside built to hold back irrigation water.*

In places the flood was 1000 metres wide. The poisons spread across rice fields and marshes and also into a small river that flowed into a national park.

Workers and local people were able to stop the poison reaching the national park by closing the floodgates. Even so, about 6000 hectares of the surrounding land was polluted, and fish, birds and other wildlife died. It will take many years to clear up the damage to the local environment.

Trees and floods

People use wood for many things, including building houses, making furniture and producing paper. In many parts of the world, people need wood for fires so that they can cook, heat water and keep themselves warm. Trees are also cut down to clear land for crops or to provide grazing for sheep, cows and other animals. But trees do not grow quickly enough to meet the demand for wood. Without the trees, soil is easily washed away and forests cannot grow back. This is called **deforestation**.

Trees and soil

In tropical climates, where there are sudden torrents of rain, tree-covered slopes help to prevent flooding and mud slides. These might otherwise destroy villages in the valleys below. Forests on hills and mountainsides also stop fertile soils washing away.

▶ *Removal of trees on hills allows soil to be washed away by heavy rains. It can also lead to flooding in low-lying areas. Poor farming methods add to the problem.*

Trees cut down

Overgrazed pastures

Growing cereal crops year after year breaks up the soil, which is then easily washed away.

Rainwater runs down furrows and forms gullies. If sloping land is ploughed rather than terraced, water gushes down more easily.

Lakes and rivers become choked with silt

▲ *This Nepalese woman is collecting firewood in the mountains. Large numbers of people uprooting bushes and trees for firewood day after day leads to serious soil erosion.*

Living sponges

In the rainy season, large amounts of rainwater fall. Tree roots soak up much of this water as it sinks into the soil. If the trees did not act as living sponges, the water could fill streams and rivers and make them overflow. The tree roots also hold the soil together. When forests are cut down there is nothing to hold the soil and it washes away. This is called **soil erosion**. The soil often ends up in rivers. It builds up there, and the rivers overflow.

Bangladesh has suffered the worst floods this century. Some of these are thought to have been caused, in part, by people cutting down forests for firewood in the mountainous country of Nepal. These include the devastating floods that struck Bangladesh in 1998.

The Philippines

In the Philippine islands of Leyte and Negros in November 1991 there was serious flooding following a tropical cyclone. Heavy rain fell on nearby slopes that had been cleared of trees. About 6000 people were killed when towns and villages were washed away by the flood water. The forests on the surrounding mountains had been cut down for firewood, for timber and to make fields to grow crops.

▼ *Soil on these treeless slopes in Portugal has been washed away in a heavy rainstorm.*

Giant sea waves

Rivers and rainfall are one cause of flooding. The sea is another. Giant sea **waves**, called **tsunamis**, cause flooding, death and destruction.

Tsunamis

Tsunamis are long, high sea waves. People often call them tidal waves, although these massive walls of water have nothing to do with the **tides**. Most tsunamis are caused by underwater earthquakes. A few occur when volcanoes under the sea erupt.

Violent vibrations

The **vibrations**, or shaking movements, of an earthquake occur when the edges of two great slabs of rock in the Earth's crust suddenly wrench apart. The place on the Earth's surface above the earthquake is called the **epicentre**. The vibrations spread out from this spot in shock waves.

High-speed waves

When an earthquake occurs under the sea, the vibrations also spread out – in waves of water. In the open sea, these may be only a

▲ *In a tsunami, a wall of water batters the coast and strong winds bend the palm trees along the shoreline.*

metre or so high. Sailors may not even notice them. But a tsunami travels hundreds, and sometimes thousands, of kilometres very fast. As it reaches shallow water, it slows down and grows enormous, reaching heights of over 60 metres.

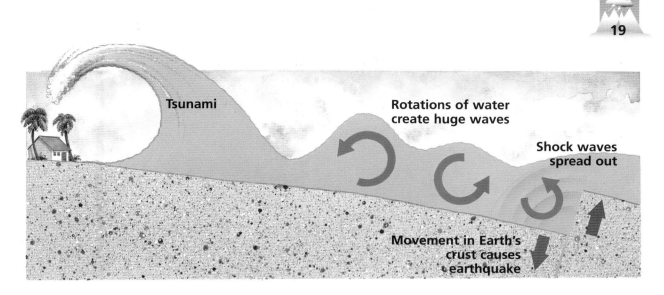

Tsunami

Rotations of water create huge waves

Shock waves spread out

Movement in Earth's crust causes earthquake

Tsunami damage

The highest tsunami ever recorded was off the coast of Japan in April 1771. It reached a staggering height of 85 metres. Another tsunami in the Sea of Japan in July 1993 swept down on the city of Okushiri. It killed 240 people and did enormous damage to houses, shops, factories and the local fishing industry. Fishing boats were snatched up by the waves and flung far inland.

A volcanic tsunami

When the volcano erupted on the island of Krakatoa in 1883, it made the loudest noise ever recorded. People in Australia, 5000 kilometres away, heard the eruption. The land shook so violently that it caused nine tsunamis that swept halfway round the world. Ships were washed ashore on the islands of the East Indies and 36 000 people died.

▲ *A tsunami can reach speeds of over 800 km/h – faster than many jet aircraft.*

▲ *A road wrecked by the tsunami that struck Okushiri, Japan, in 1993.*

Storm surges

◄ *Large areas of Bangladesh are at or only just above sea level. They are regularly flooded by storm surges.*

Coastal flooding can also be caused by **storm surges**. A storm surge is a sudden rise in sea level. It is produced when water is piled up against the coast by strong winds blowing towards the land. The water may rise as much as 5 metres above normal high-tide levels. Storm surges result in widespread flooding, extensive damage and serious loss of life.

Storm surges are common in the Gulf of Mexico and along the Atlantic coast of the United States. They also occur around the islands of the western Pacific, where typhoons are common, in the Bay of Bengal and along the shores of the North Sea.

Surges and cyclones

The nation of Bangladesh is particularly prone to storm surges. Only a quarter of Bangladesh lies more than 3 metres above sea level, yet 117 million people live there. More people have lost their lives in storm surges in Bangladesh than anywhere else on Earth. This is because Bangladesh is often hit by tropical storms called cyclones.

Surge disasters

In April 1991, the surface of the sea off Bangladesh was whipped up by a tropical cyclone until it was some 6 metres higher than normal. This surge swept over low-lying areas of Bangladesh, causing great damage.

► *Flood waters engulf this house in Dhaka, the capital of Bangladesh.*

The surge killed 140 000 people, and left millions more homeless.

In May 1997, another tropical cyclone struck Bangladesh. It was just as powerful as the 1991 storm, and destroyed or damaged about 400 000 homes. This time, though, the death toll was much smaller, with about 200 people being killed. Many lives were saved because better warnings of the storm had been given and people were able to take refuge in the special cyclone shelters that had been built after the 1991 disaster.

Western India

Another tropical cyclone struck western India in June 1998, again causing enormous storm surges. The area worst affected was a so-called shanty town. This was a town where the poorest people lived in flimsy houses made from cardboard, corrugated iron, scrap wood and other waste materials. Blown by winds gusting at up to 185 km/h, the sea surge swept the shanty town away, killing many of the people. We may never know how many people died because many of the bodies were swept out to sea.

▼ *To prevent storm surges flooding London, a barrier was built across the River Thames. The barrier is raised when tidal surges and storm floods are likely.*

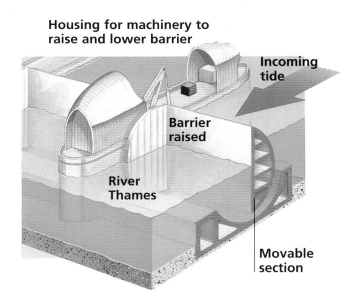

Housing for machinery to raise and lower barrier

Incoming tide

Barrier raised

River Thames

Movable section

Sinking cities

Many great cities grew up around trading ports and lie close to sea level. These are at risk of flooding. Even worse, some cities and parts of countries are slowly sinking, which means they are even more likely to flood in the future.

Double trouble

Bangkok, the capital of Thailand, is built on the low-lying flood plain of the Chao Phraya River, about 25 kilometres from the sea. The people of Bangkok obtain their water for drinking, washing and cooking from wells sunk into the

▼ Bangkok, like many of the world's greatest cities, lies close to sea level and often floods.

ground. The rocks under the city are soft clays and sands. As water is drawn from the 10 000 or more wells that pass through these rocks, the rocks dry out and shrink.

As the rocks shrink, Bangkok sinks, in some places at a rate of about 14 centimetres per year. If this continues, in just a few years the entire city will be below sea level. Bangkok will be flooded by both the sea and the river.

◄ Venice is sinking because too much water is being taken from under the city and because the sea level is rising.

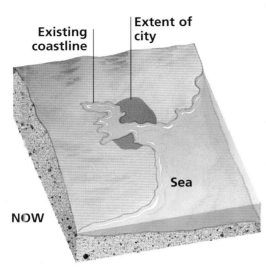

Existing coastline

Extent of city

Sea

NOW

▼ *If an area of land under a city gradually sinks and the sea level rises, much of the city could become permanently flooded.*

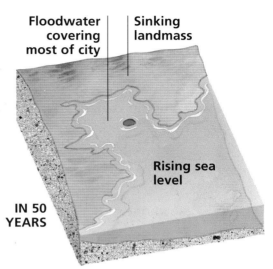

Floodwater covering most of city

Sinking landmass

Rising sea level

IN 50 YEARS

Venice and Tokyo

A similar disaster is threatening the Italian city of Venice, which is on the shores of the Adriatic Sea. Because too much water has been taken from the ground, the city has sunk by about 12.5 centimetres in the last 50 years. At the same time, the Adriatic Sea has risen by about 9 centimetres. Venice now floods whenever there is a high tide combined with heavy rainfall and a storm surge.

Tokyo, the capital of Japan, is sinking by about 15 centimetres a year because of similar overuse of water. The city could be in even greater danger than Bangkok and Venice because it is in the Pacific. This area is often affected by earthquakes and typhoons.

Seesaw lands

When the ice melted after the last **Ice Age**, lands that were previously covered by huge ice sheets were freed from an enormous weight. The land started to spring back up extremely slowly, like a seesaw, and this is still going on today. The northwest corner of North America is rising by about 20 millimetres a year, while the northwest corner of the British Isles is rising by about 12 millimetres a year.

At the same time, the opposite corners – Louisiana and Texas in the United States, and the southeast of England in the British Isles – are sinking. As they sink, they become more at risk of flooding by the sea.

Coastal defences

The best barriers against flooding from the sea are natural defences, such as beaches, **sand dunes** and **salt marshes**. Unfortunately, these are all easily damaged by the growth of towns, seaside resorts, industries and other human activities. So huge sums of money are spent on building artificial sea defences. These are man-made ways of trying to hold back the sea so that it does not damage the land along the shore.

Sea walls

Sometimes, a sea wall is built. Some sea walls are simply high banks of soil, sand or stones. Often, plants are grown on top of the wall to

▲ Large chunks of rock have been placed in front of this sea wall in Portugal to break up the force of the waves.

help to hold it together. More often, a concrete sea wall is built. This may be curved or stepped. A curved wall pushes the waves up, round and back out to sea again. Whatever the design, sea walls stop damage to the coast, as well as preventing flooding.

Most scientists agree that the best place for sea walls is on the landward side of natural defences such as beaches and salt marshes. This gives the coast a double line of protection.

◄ A wooden groyne prevents the pebbles on this beach being sucked away into the sea.

Fence defence

Groynes are fences built on beaches at right angles to the sea. They slow down the waves and stop sand and pebbles from being washed away from the beach. They help to keep the beach in place for people to use and also help to protect the land from the sea.

Breakwaters

Breakwaters are long barriers of large boulders or concrete shapes built out into the sea. These break up the force of the waves before they reach the shore. Breakwaters also protect boats and ships in harbours from damage in stormy weather. In a few places, artificial **reefs** of concrete or stone are built in the sea parallel to the shore. These also break up the force of the waves before they can reach the shore and cause damage to harbours and the coastline.

Sand dunes

If the wind blows towards a sandy shore for most of the year, it may pile up the sand to form hills called sand dunes. Like beaches and salt marshes, sand dunes are a natural sea defence. But sand dunes are easily damaged by people walking over them. The sand in the dune may then be blown away again when a strong wind blows. To stop this happening, people plant special grasses or trees on sand dunes to help to hold them in place.

▼ *Breakwaters and groynes slow the waves and prevent the erosion of the beach. Grasses, too, hold the beach in place as a barrier against the waves. A sea wall provides a last line of defence.*

Sand dunes

Salt marshes

Sea wall

Beach

Wooden groyne

Concrete breakwater

Waves

River defences

There are also ways of stopping river floods. As we have seen, a river floods when heavy rain, melting snow, or a storm surge produces more water than the river can hold. It may flood because it is blocked by ice.

Levees

Rivers carry lots of mud and sand in their waters. These tiny pieces of rock have been worn away from the sides and bottom of the river on its way down from the hills or mountains where it began.

In the lower course of a river, where the water flows more slowly, it drops much of the mud and sand it has been carrying. This **debris** raises the river bed.

This is happening in the Mississippi River in the United States. As the bed of the Mississippi rises, people living near it have built high banks, called **levees**, to stop the river flooding their homes. In the last 100 years, people have built up parts of the river bank by more than 6 metres.

Digging deep

Another way to reduce the risk of flooding is to use a special kind of ship, called a dredger, to remove mud and sand from the river bed. This deepens the river so that it can hold more water.

Some rivers wind from side to side, or meander, in their lower parts. This slows down the water and causes flooding. Straightening the channel so that the water flows quickly out to sea can help prevent flooding. Unfortunately, this makes the river less suitable as a home for water plants and animals.

▼ *The River Mississippi broke through these earth embankments, or levees, and flooded the surrounding farmland.*

◄ *This dredger is removing sand and mud from the bottom of a Dutch river. Making the river deeper means that it can hold more water, and will not be so likely to flood.*

Sometimes a relief channel can be dug to divert some of the flood water away from the main river. Planting trees on steep slopes near rivers slows the rate at which water flows down the slopes and into the river. It also helps to hold the soil in place and stops it being washed into the river.

Holding back

Some flooding can be prevented by building dams or sluice gates. These hold back and store water in artificial lakes, or reservoirs, then let it go slowly. The new Three Gorges Dam, built to control flooding of the Yangtze River in China, will hold back a 600-kilometre-long reservoir. Flood barriers are another means of defence. They are built across **estuaries** to protect the towns upstream from storm surges.

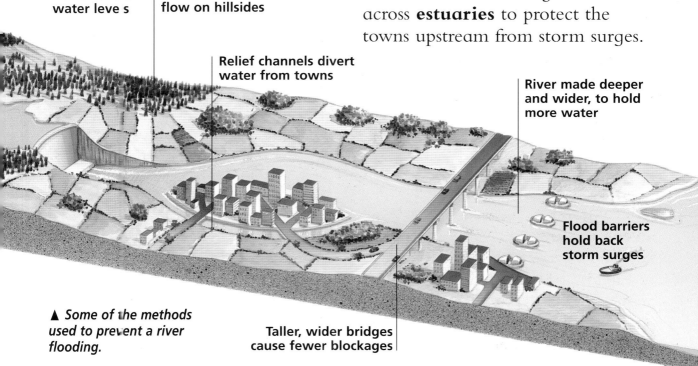

Dams control water levels

Trees slow water flow on hillsides

Relief channels divert water from towns

River made deeper and wider, to hold more water

Flood barriers hold back storm surges

▲ *Some of the methods used to prevent a river flooding.*

Taller, wider bridges cause fewer blockages

A flooded world

Everywhere in the world, the climate is changing. Many places that are tropical today were once covered in ice. In the past, these changes happened very slowly, over many thousands of years. Today, however, people may be making the climate change more quickly than ever before. One reason is that we are putting more and more carbon dioxide into the atmosphere.

The greenhouse effect

Carbon dioxide comes mainly from car exhausts, from power stations and factories, and from burning forests to clear land for farming.

In normal amounts, carbon dioxide does a useful job. It is sometimes called a greenhouse gas, because it forms a layer over the Earth, that stops heat from the Sun from rising back into space.

But now there are too many greenhouse gases. Too much of the sun's energy is being trapped and the world is warming up. This is called the **greenhouse effect**.

Earth's atmosphere contains gases such as carbon dioxide

Heat trapped in the atmosphere

Some heat escapes

A portion of the Sun's heat enters Earth's atmosphere (most is reflected)

Sun

Earth

◄ *The Earth's temperature is controlled by the amount of the sun's heat reaching the ground and the amount of heat escaping from the Earth into space.*

▶ When power stations burn fuels, such as coal, to produce electricity, they put large amounts of carbon dioxide and other pollution into the air.

Rising temperatures

Already the average world temperature has risen by more than 1°C since 1850. Many scientists think that the average temperature of the world could rise by another 2°C by the year 2100. If this happens, the huge layers of ice and snow at the North and South Poles will begin to melt. The water in the oceans will also expand, or take up more space, as it warms up. This could cause sea levels to rise by about 50 centimetres. Low-lying areas, including many of the world's largest cities, may be flooded.

▲ Trees take in carbon dioxide from the air and give out oxygen. So planting trees is one way of helping to reduce the greenhouse effect.

What can we do?

Everyone can do something to reduce the greenhouse effect.

Do not waste paper, because paper comes from trees, which take in lots of carbon dioxide from the air. Take old paper and newspapers to a recycling bin.

Recycle glass, metals and other materials, too. Factories produce a lot of carbon dioxide when they make these materials for us.

Walk or cycle short distances, or travel by bus, train or tram if you can. This produces less pollution per person than travelling by car.

Do not waste electricity or other kinds of energy. When electricity is made, huge quantities of carbon dioxide are pumped into the air.

Glossary

alluvial soil A fertile soil formed from the mud and sand carried by rivers.

bank The raised or sloping ground beside a river, canal or lake.

beach The place where the water of a sea or lake meets the land. A beach is made of pebbles or sand.

breakwater A wall of concrete or stones built at a right angle to the shore. It stops the beach being washed away by the sea.

climate The average weather of a region of the Earth throughout the year.

dam A large wall or bank built to hold back water and to raise its level. A reservoir often forms behind the dam.

debris Rubbish carried along by a river. Debris can include silt, sand, rocks, litter or even whole tree trunks.

deforestation When forests are cut down by people and not replanted.

delta An area of flat land at the mouth, or estuary, of a river, created by mud and sand dumped there by the river. Many deltas are shaped like a fan or triangle.

earthquake A violent shaking of the ground caused by movements of the rocks in the Earth's crust.

epicentre The point on the Earth's crust that lies above the centre of an earthquake.

estuary The wide mouth of a river where fresh water meets sea water.

fertile Land that is fertile has a rich soil and produces good crops.

flood When water spills over on to the land from a river, lake or sea.

flood plain The flat land near a river which floods after heavy rain.

greenhouse effect The warming of the Earth caused by gases such as carbon dioxide in the air. These gases reduce the amount of the sun's heat that escapes into space.

groyne A fence built at a right angle to the shore. It stops the beach being washed away by the sea.

hurricane A powerful, swirling storm found in tropical parts of the Atlantic Ocean. Such storms are called cylones or typhoons in Asia and willy-willies in Australia.

Ice Age A time of extreme cold that began about a million years ago and ended 10 000 years ago.

impermeable Describes any material that does not let liquids and gases pass through.

irrigation Supplying water to farmland, usually by building canals and ditches.

lake A large area of fresh or salt water surrounded by land.

levee A river bank made from material dumped by a river when it floods. People build levees to keep a river in its channel and so prevent floods.

meander A large, S-shaped bend in a river.

monsoon A wind that brings heavy rain. The strongest blows from the Indian Ocean in summer, bringing rains to southern Asia.

permeable Describes any material that lets liquids and gases pass through it.

reef A line of rocks near the surface of the sea.

reservoir A large lake built by people to store water for drinking, for producing electricity or for watering crops. A reservoir can also be used to hold back water behind a dam, so that its flow is controlled.

salt marsh Mud banks at the mouth, or estuary, of a river where fresh and salt water meet. Certain plants that can withstand salt and fresh water grow there.

sand dune A hill of sand formed by the blowing of the wind.

soil erosion The gradual removal of topsoil from an area of land by flowing water, rain or wind.

storm surge The sudden rise in sea level when strong winds blow a high tide towards the land.

tides The rise and fall of the oceans and seas twice a day. Tides are produced by the pulling effect of the moon and sun on the oceans and seas.

tsunami A large sea wave, usually caused by an earthquake or volcano on the sea bed.

valley A low-lying strip of land between steep hills or mountains. A river or stream may run along the bottom of the valley.

vibration A rapid to-and-fro movement.

volcano A hole or tear in the Earth's crust from which molten rock, called lava, flows.

wave A regular movement of the surface of water caused by the wind.

Index